A Gift

Presented to

_____

Given by

_____

Date

_____

What Others Say...

There is a Proverb that says a merry heart does good like a medicine. What a better way to handle the stresses of married life than to insert humor into the practical difficulties that all couples face from time to time. Maybe all of us could benefit by stepping back and laughing a little bit. It is my privilege to endorse *Sweeties Manual* because of the example that is set forth in the daily lives of the authors.

Dale Blair, Pastor

In my profession of counseling rarely are there any books that promote respect, humor, and passion in your marriage. Well my friends, I have finally found one named *Sweeties Manual* that walks you through the steps of building a healthy marriage and having fun while doing it. There are many hilarious illustrations that will make you aware and chuckle at some of the pitfalls in your marriage that need to be addressed. It's such a great read and a nice gift for any married (or about to be married) couple you may know. Order one today; you'll be glad you did.

Dr. Michael Brooks
Applicable Counseling & Coaching Services
(applicablecoaching.com)
Denver, Colorado

This book contains a wealth of very practical suggestions about marriage gleaned by the authors from years of experience. The *Sweeties Manual* presents timely advice about how to relate to your partner through a delightful combination of wit and wisdom. It is an excellent resource for any married or about-to-be married couple.

Henry M. Brown, PH.D.
Former Associate Professor of English and Tennis Coach
Furman University; Greenville, South Carolina

Matrimonial wisdom masquerading as whimsy, each vignette of the *Sweeties Manual* echoes a back-story that stretches back to the Garden. A deceptive delight: one moment you're paddling in the shallows then all of a sudden you're up to your neck in some pretty stormy seas.

Best-selling author David Crossman

SWEETIES
MANUAL

DAVID & TRISH RICHARDSON

Design and Illustration by
JIM & FRIEDA BAIRD

CREATION
HOUSE

Sweeties Manual
by David and Trish Richardson
Published by Creation House
A Charisma Media Company
600 Rinehart Road
Lake Mary, Florida 32746
www.charismamedia.com

Unless otherwise noted, all Scripture quotations are from the New King James Version of the Bible. Copyright © 1979, 1980, 1982 by Thomas Nelson, Inc., publishers. Used by permission.

Design Director: Justin Evans
Cover design by Rachel Lopez
Illustrators: Jim and Frieda Baird

Visit the author's website: www.TheSweeties.com

Library of Congress Cataloging-in-Publication Data: 2016938853
International Standard Book Number: 978-1-62998-546-6
E-book International Standard Book Number: 978-1-62998-547-3

While the authors have made every effort to provide accurate mailing and Internet addresses at the time of publication, neither the publisher nor the authors assume any responsibility for errors or for changes that occur after publication.

First edition

16 17 18 19 20—9 8 7 6 5 4 3 2 1
Printed in China

Our Deepest Appreciation For...

Our Lord Jesus Christ.

All people who love to laugh,
with the courage to laugh at themselves;
who seek the good in others;
who know this is a wonderful life
to be lived and treasured.

The Sweeties celebrate you!

Contents

Introduction
From Trish and David
"I guess we're not Sweeties anymore!
You can find it in the Sweeties Manual!"

Hurt and sobbing, I cried out those words to David during one of our trivial albeit tense and contentious moments one Sunday afternoon in May 1986. That declaration became just the first of many "Sweeties Moments" which we committed to pen and paper for future reference...not realizing the personal and awe-inspiring journey we were destined to embark upon.

Statistically speaking, 100 percent of all marriages begin with some form of a wedding—a ceremony that marks the beginning of what should be two dear hearts overflowing with astounding love for each other. In this mindset, Trish and I began our "adventure" in the summer of 1983 ready to discover how we could, through fun and personal challenge, take our relationship to bright, new, amazing levels!

Several years later we were blessed to meet a wonderful couple, Jim and Frieda Baird, who became such a tremendously intricate part of bringing life to the *Sweeties Manual.*

From Frieda and Jim
"Frieda, see what you can do with this."

Discovering I wrote the spiritual growth and development book *Do Yourself a Favor,* David handed a folder to me containing many type written sheets with catchy expressions of wisdom. Jim and I knew this was a treasure that needed to be visualized.

Later, staring at blank sheets of paper, Jim, an experienced artist and illustrator, prayed, "Please, God, help me with this." Not long after, images began to form in his mind from which he developed the first *Sweeties* caricatures that appear on the cover of the *Sweeties Manual.*

Through many dinners, toilsome hours and late nights, through energy and fatigue, the four of us discussed the limitless possibilities of bringing these unique literary concepts to life with illustrations. In time, along with lots of prayer and collaboration, Jim and I created the unique design and humorous "tongue-in-cheek" illustrations, combined with the visual concept and logo to embellish the expressive maxims.

The "Sweeties Manual" is born!

Designed and created for all couples whether preparing for marriage or those already married for an hour or ninety-nine years. Be prepared to laugh, to cry, to make a revealing personal change, perhaps to learn what or what not to do, but most importantly share in this incredible journey as you see your own marriage reflected in each "Sweeties Moment."

An amazing gift of love that is timeless…you will want to give this true and delightfully whimsical book to every married (or about to be married) couple you know. The colorful and entertaining "tongue-and-cheek" illustrations, along with each enchanting expression of wisdom, will *forever* be a constant source of guidance, inspiration, comfort, conviction, hope, and above all *Love*.

For Better or For Worse…let love begin and
always remain in our own hearts…
Forever Together!

Blessings Always,
The Sweeties

P.S. Don't forget to look for the adorable 'Sweeties' mice.

*S*weeties
go on picnics
together...
even in the winter.

*S*weeties attend plays together.

NOTABLES

Sweeties are the beating of two hearts into one.

*S*weeties
look their best
when they
go out
for the evening.

Give special
attention when
your Sweetie
doesn't feel well.

Do fun
and exciting
things with your
Sweetie.

sweeties
NOTABLES

Let every kiss given to your Sweetie
have the magic of your very first.

Loving your Sweetie should be like breathing.

Dance
the night away
with
your Sweetie.

*S*weeties
always work to
better their
relationship.

*S*weeties
enjoy working out
together.

NOTABLES

Love always forgives.

_____

_____

_____

_____

_____

_____

_____

_____

_____

_____

_____

_____

_____

_____

_____

_____

_____

_____

Know your Sweetie's greatest hopes and dreams.

*T*ake
healthy jogs
with your
Sweetie.

*I*ron clothes
when your
Sweetie is late.

NOTABLES

Let your relationship with your Sweetie go
far beyond great—make it *Amazing!*

Sweeties honor each other in every way.

*F*ind humor
each day...
but never at
your Sweetie's
expense.

*S*weeties
attend their place
of worship
together.

*S*weeties spend private, romantic evenings together.

*N*ever
lose patience
with your
Sweetie.

NOTABLES

Commit to loving your Sweetie with
all your heart, mind, body, and soul.

Show how prized your Sweetie is above all others.

*S*weeties show
their emotions
together.

*N*ever
do anything
to lose your
Sweetie's trust.

*S*weeties plan
their future
carefully.

Sweeties
NOTABLES

_____

_____

_____

_____

_____

_____

_____

_____

_____

_____

_____

_____

_____

_____

_____

Invest your time, money, and energy into your
Sweetie. Your heart will follow you there.

Sweeties strive to understand and
practice unconditional love.

*S*nuggle on the sofa with your Sweetie, like before you were married.

Share your
popcorn and
drink with
your Sweetie.

*S*weeties
always forgive
and say,
"I'm sorry."

65

sweeties
NOTABLES

Daily remind your Sweetie,
"You are *one* in a *million* to me!"

Sweeties always show a respectful heart.

Sweeties never lose appeal for one another.

Do something
extra loving
when your
Sweetie is stressed.

*T*reasure those
tender moments
with your
Sweetie.

*S*weeties
meet in
special,
secret places.

*T*urn off the TV
and share
your dreams
with your Sweetie.

NOTABLES

Fall in love with your Sweetie every single day.

Call just to hear your Sweetie's voice.

*T*ell your Sweetie
how beautiful
she looks
without makeup.

Help your Sweetie bring in the groceries.

NOTABLES

Be your Sweetie's best friend and forever soul mate.

Sweeties really listen when sharing personal
thoughts and feelings. Make each other feel safe.

Put
the toilet lid
down for
your Sweetie.

$\mathcal{F}$ill up
your Sweetie's car
with gas.

*S*weeties enjoy
sporting events
together.

NOTABLES

Create an amazing, never-ending
story with your Sweetie.

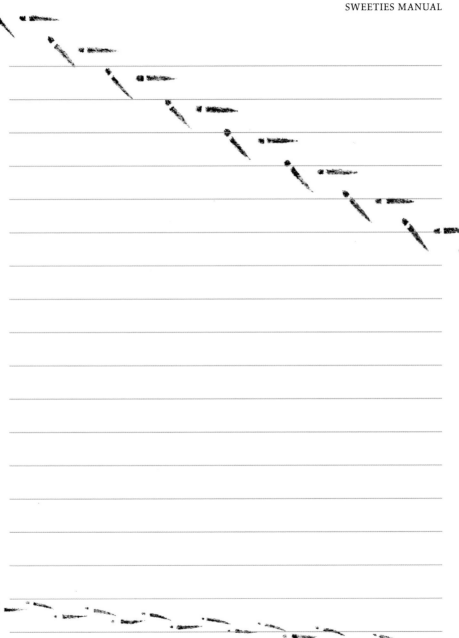

Remember to tell just how special your Sweetie is to you.

Romance your
Sweetie with
a poem.

Wash your
Sweetie's car
without
being asked.

NOTABLES

Sweeties have a communicative heart.

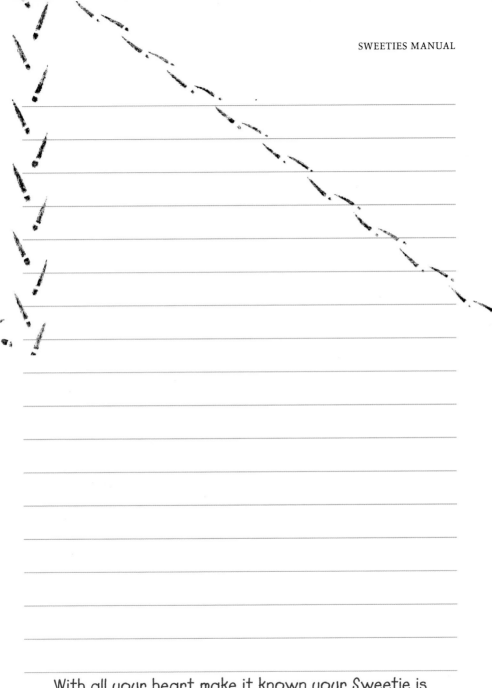

With all your heart make it known your Sweetie is
the very best thing that ever happened to you.

Smell sweet for your Sweetie.

*S*weeties only
have eyes
for each other.

NOTABLES

Dance with your Sweetie like no one
or everyone is watching.

Tell your Sweetie, "I would marry you all over again."

Share your
secret thoughts
with
your Sweetie.

*H*ave a meal
prepared
when your
Sweetie
arrives home
tired
from work.

Respect
your Sweetie's
opinions…
right or wrong.

NOTABLES

Never let the sun go down without giving
your Sweetie a good night kiss.

Give a passionate kiss when your
Sweetie least expects it.

*S*weeties
sit together
on the
same side
of the booth.

*B*e Sweetie's
prince and slay
those dragons.

NOTABLES

Never, ever forget…of all the Sweeties
in the world, yours chose *you!*

Forever Sweeties, our stories never end.

NOTABLES

_____

_____

_____

_____

_____

_____

_____

_____

_____

_____

_____

_____

_____

_____

_____

_____

NOTABLES

_____

_____

_____

_____

_____

_____

_____

_____

_____

_____

_____

_____

_____

_____

_____

_____

_____

NOTABLES

_____

_____

_____

_____

_____

_____

_____

_____

_____

_____

_____

_____

_____

_____

_____

_____

_____

The Authors...

DAVID AND TRISH RICHARDSON

Having first laid eyes on each other in the Fall of 1982 in Charlotte, NC, David and Trish had no idea how many extraordinary chapters they would create in their lives together. Becoming 'Sweeties' has truly been a life-changing process—from their wedding in 1983, being blessed to raise three incredible sons to the day they finished writing the *Sweeties Manual*. As each day follows, it continues to be a journey like none other. Such an AMAZING blend of love, honor, respect, and grace.

David and Trish are the proud parents of sons, Frank, Brian and Brett, their beautiful wives Emily, Kelli, and Pam and cherished grandchildren, Samantha, Matthew, Taylor, Christian, Austin, Haylee and Hunter and last but not least, their beloved Maltese, Mr. Big (small in stature but LOTS of attitude!)

The Artists...

JIM AND FRIEDA BAIRD

Jim, an ordained minister, has decades of experience as an illustrator/graphic artist. His advertisements have appeared in several national publications plus numerous newspapers across the country. Jim's work includes a portrait of Miss America, which he formally presented to her at the National Press Club in Washington, DC. In addition, he presented Pat Robertson, founder of CBN and the 700 Club, with a portrait.

Frieda is the published author of *Do Yourself a Favor*, the first book from her *Let Us Remember* series, as well as the to be released *You Watched Me Disappear.*

Jim and Frieda are the proud parents of Victor and Dawne, daughter-in-law, Emily and precious grandchildren Amber and Ethan.

Contact the Authors

Blythe Co., Inc.

blythecorp@aol.com

Please visit us at www.TheSweeties.com